WITHDRAWN
FROM STOCK

BIRDS
PREDATORS

Written by
Mignonne Gunasekara

BookLife
PUBLISHING

©2020
BookLife Publishing Ltd.
King's Lynn
Norfolk PE30 4LS

ISBN: 978-1-83927-258-5

Written by:
Mignonne Gunasekara

Edited by:
Shalini Vallepur

Designed by:
Amy Li

A catalogue record for this book is available from the British Library.

All facts, statistics, web addresses and URLs in this book were verified as valid and accurate at time of writing. No responsibility for any changes to external websites or references can be accepted by either the author or publisher.

All rights reserved.
Printed in Malaysia.

CONTENTS

Page 4	Meet the Predators
Page 6	Red Kite
Page 8	Great Skua
Page 10	Barn Owl
Page 12	Common Kingfisher
Page 14	Bald Eagle
Page 16	Great White Pelican
Page 18	Peregrine Falcon
Page 20	Common Kestrel
Page 22	Spread Your Wings
Page 24	Glossary and Index

Words that look like <u>this</u> can be found in the glossary on page 24.

MEET THE PREDATORS

Welcome to the world of predators. Predators are animals that hunt other animals for food. They come in many shapes and sizes, but they all have something in common — to their prey, they are terrifying!

In this book, we will be looking at predators that are birds. They might look beautiful but don't be fooled – they rule the skies as well as the roost.

A roost is where birds go to rest or sleep.

RED KITE

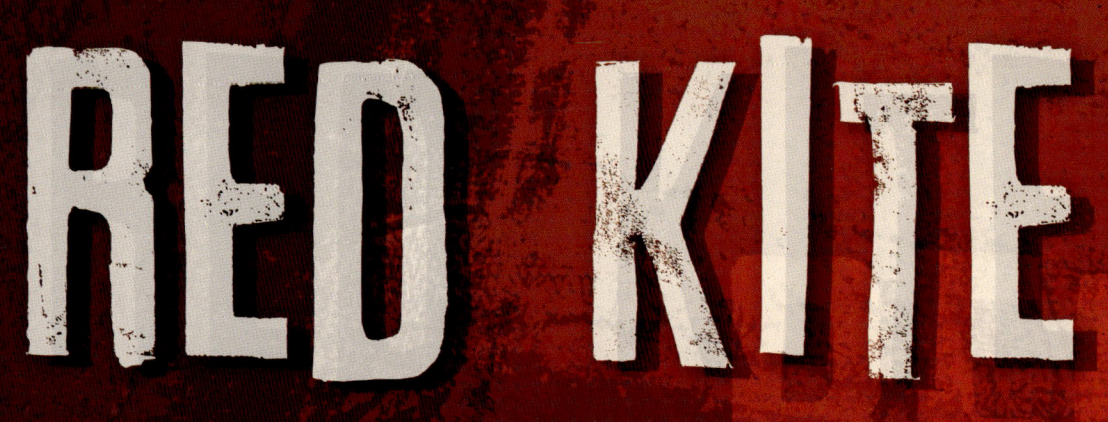

Many red kites were killed by humans in the past and the species nearly went extinct in the UK. However, their numbers are doing better now.

Hooked beak

A species is a group of very similar animals that can have babies together.

Red kites are scavengers. They eat animals that are already dead, called <u>carrion</u>. They sometimes hunt for small animals, such as rabbits.

Fact File

<u>Habitat</u>: Woodland, open areas

<u>Weapons</u>: Hooked beak

<u>Prey</u>: Worms, small <u>mammals</u>, carrion

Red kites usually eat whatever prey they can find.

GREAT SKUA

The great skua is known as a 'pirate of the sea'. This is because great skuas steal food from other birds.

The great skua is also known as the bonxie.

Sharp beak

Great skuas eat smaller birds, such as puffins.

The great skua is a large seabird. It has been known to fly angrily at anyone that gets too close to its nest.

Fact File

Habitat: Coast, moorland

Weapons: Sharp beak, talons

Prey: Fish, birds, carrion

BARN OWL

Barn owls have very good hearing to help them hunt at night. The shape of their face helps them to hear by sending sounds past their ears.

Barn owls can fly very quietly to sneak up on prey.

Hooked beak

Sharp talons

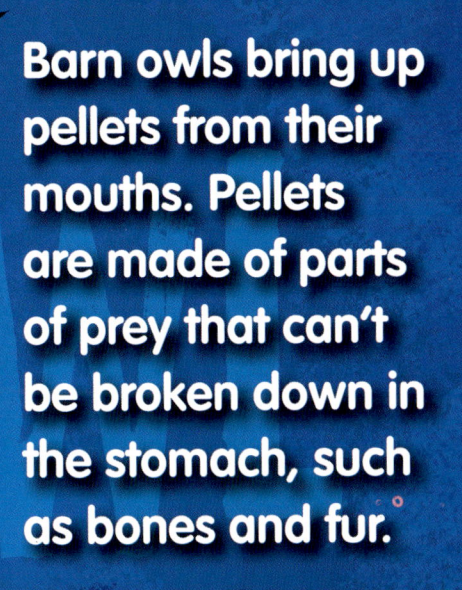

Barn owls bring up pellets from their mouths. Pellets are made of parts of prey that can't be broken down in the stomach, such as bones and fur.

Barn owls eat small mammals, such as voles and mice.

Pellet

Fact File

Habitat: Farmland, grassland, wetland, coast

Weapons: Good hearing, sharp talons

Prey: Shrews, field voles, wood mice

COMMON KINGFISHER

These small, colourful birds can be found fishing near rivers and other slow-moving waters. They mostly hunt for small fish, but they also eat insects.

Perch

Perches are where birds can rest or get a good look around.

Common kingfishers hunt by sitting on perches near water, where prey is easy to spot. They dive into the water to catch prey and bring it back to their perch to eat.

Quick flyer

The common kingfisher eats shrimp.

Fact File

Habitat: Grassland, wetland

Weapons: Speed

Prey: Fish, insects, shrimp

BALD EAGLE

Bald eagles belong to a group of birds known as sea eagles. They have very good eyesight and can see prey from far away.

Hooked beak

Bald eagles have sharp, hooked beaks to rip into food.

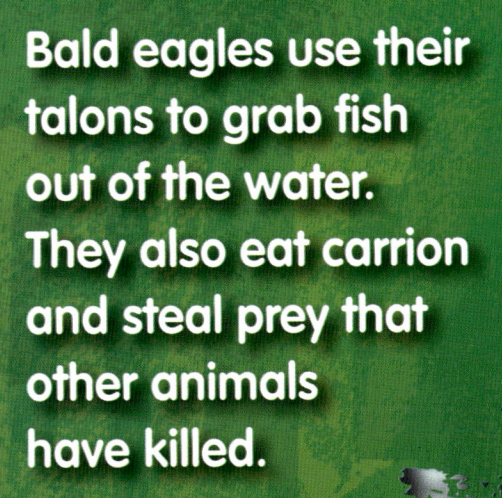

Bald eagles use their talons to grab fish out of the water. They also eat carrion and steal prey that other animals have killed.

Bald eagles eat a lot of fish, such as salmon.

Sharp talons

Fact File

Habitat: Wetland, grassland

Weapons: Good eyesight, talons, sharp beak

Prey: Fish, small mammals, other birds

15

GREAT WHITE PELICAN

Pelicans are some of the largest birds on Earth. They are known for the stretchy pouches under their bills, which they use to scoop fish out of the water.

Pelicans have webbed feet to help them swim.

Large bill

Throat pouch

Webbed feet

16

Great white pelicans usually fish in groups. They swim together and push the fish into one area, then scoop them up to eat.

Pelicans can fly for long distances to look for food.

Fact File

Habitat: Wetland

Weapons: Bill, hunting in groups

Prey: Fish

PEREGRINE FALCON

Peregrine falcons can be found everywhere, from cliffs by the sea to tall buildings in cities. A peregrine falcon's main prey is birds.

Peregrine falcons hunt prey such as pigeons.

Pointed wings

Talons

They grab prey out of the air with their talons.

Peregrine falcons hunt by diving at their prey while flying. They can reach speeds of over 300 kilometres per hour while diving!

Fact File

Habitat: Most places except Antarctica

Weapons: Talons, speed

Prey: Mostly birds, bats

COMMON KESTREL

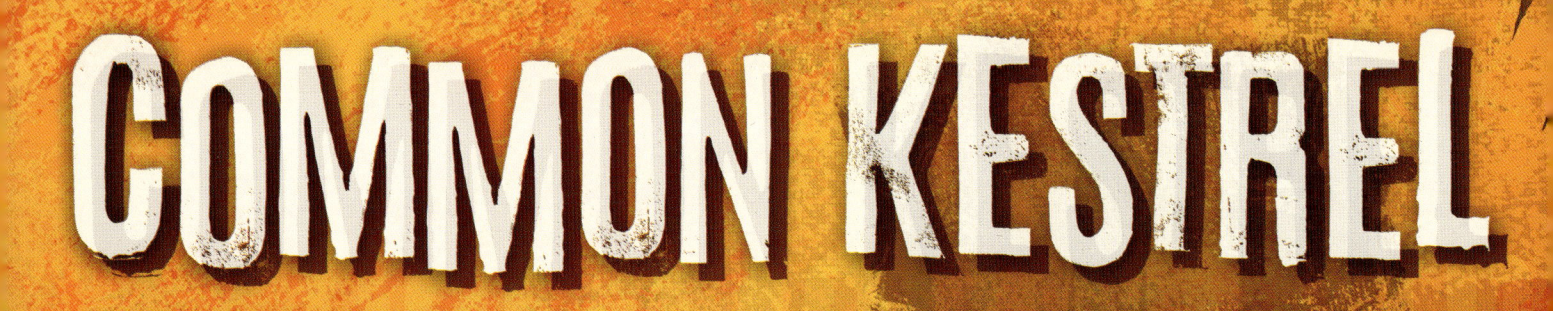

Hovering makes it easier for the common kestrel to see and catch their prey.

Sharp talons

Common kestrels have an interesting way of hunting. They can stay in one place in the air while flying. This is called hovering.

20

Sharp beak

Common kestrels can be found in many habitats. They eat small mammals such as voles, mice and shrews. In towns and cities, common kestrels may find it easier to eat birds than mammals.

Common kestrels mainly eat voles. They sometimes eat insects and worms.

Fact File

Habitat: Farmland, grassland, towns and cities

Weapons: Talons, good eyesight

Prey: Small mammals, small birds, insects, worms

SPREAD YOUR WINGS

Congratulations, you met the predators! Weren't they fierce? Let's see them stretch their wings and fly!

Which bird has the biggest wingspan?

185 centimetres

Common kingfisher

Red kite

25 centimetres

22

Peregrine falcon

89 centimetres

Barn owl

110 centimetres

Bald eagle

250 centimetres

A wingspan is the greatest distance between the tips of an animal's wings.

GLOSSARY

bills	birds' beaks
carrion	rotting parts of dead animals
extinct	no longer existing
grassland	an area of land where grass is the main plant that grows there
habitat	the natural home in which animals, plants and other living things live
mammals	animals that are warm-blooded, have a backbone and make milk to feed their babies
moorland	an open area where rough grass grows
prey	animals that are hunted by other animals for food
talons	claws, especially those belonging to birds of prey
wetland	an area of land that is very wet or covered in water

INDEX

beaks 6–10, 14–15, 21
carrion 7, 9, 15
diving 13, 19
eyesight 14–15, 21
fish 9, 12–13, 15–17
flying 9–10, 13, 17, 19–20, 22

habitats 7, 9, 11, 13, 15, 17, 19, 21
hunting 4, 7, 10, 12–13, 17–20
insects 12–13, 21
perches 12–13

prey 4, 7, 9–21
stealing 8, 15
talons 9–11, 15, 18–21
voles 11, 21
worms 7, 21

Photo Credits. All images courtesy of Shutterstock. With thanks to Getty Images, Thinkstock Photo and iStockphoto.
Recurring images – Ameena Matcha (old paper), teacept (header font), Alexey Pushkin (grunge texture), MrNoe (claw marks), Olga_C, Grafica (grunge shapes). Cover – Martin Dallaire, silky, p2–3 – Martin Dallaire, p4–5 – Ondrej Prosicky, Rudmer Zwerver, p6–7 – Sergey Uryadnikov, Alta Oosthuizen, p8–9 – fernando sanchez, Jesus Giraldo Gutierrez, p10–11 – MZPHOTO.CZ, Mark Bridger, TheRocky41, p12–13 – Geza Kurka Photos, Christopher P McLeod, p14–15 – Brian E Kushner, Chris Hill, Sekar B, p16–17 – Vadim Petrakov, Wang LiQiang, p18–19 – Harry Collins Photography, Studioimagen73, p20–21 – Jose Paulo Xavier Diogo, Milan Zygmunt, p22–23 – FloriaStock, Geza Kurka Photos, Harry Collins Photography, Mark Medcalf, Werner Baumgarten